ESSENTIA

Motivating
People

MIKE BOURNE & PIPPA BOURNE

London, New York,
Munich, Melbourne, Delhi

Editor Daniel Mills
Senior Art Editor Helen Spencer
Production Editor Ben Marcus
Production Controller Hema Gohil
Executive Managing Editor Adèle Hayward
Managing Art Editor Kat Mead
Art Director Peter Luff
Publisher Stephanie Jackson

DK DELHI
Editor Saloni Talwar
Designer Ivy Roy
Design Manager Arunesh Talapatra
DTP Designer Pushpak Tyagi

First published in 2009 by
Dorling Kindersley Limited
80 Strand
London WC2R 0RL
A Penguin Company

2 4 6 8 10 9 7 5 3 1

Copyright © 2009
Dorling Kindersley Limited
All rights reserved

A CIP catalogue record for this book
is available from the British Library.

ISBN 978-1-4053-3687-1

Colour reproduction by
Colourscan, Singapore
Printed in China by WKT

See our complete catalogue at
www.dk.com

Contents

CHAPTER 2

Building processes for motivation

CHAPTER 3

Developing the skills of motivation

CHAPTER 4

Motivating in difficult situations

Introduction

Enthusiastic and motivated people are essential for an organization to be successful. A business with motivated staff has an advantage over its competitors. It is easier and quicker for a competitor to copy an idea for a product or service than it is for them to build a well-motivated workforce.

People now have greater expectations of their employers. They no longer expect to stay with one employer for more than a few years and may even have several different career paths during their working lives. If a skilled worker is unhappy with their employer, they will be able to change jobs without much difficulty. It is often the best people who are able to leave most quickly, making the art of motivation more important than ever.

Motivating People is divided into four sections. The first deals with the essence of motivation: what it is and how you can create the right environment for a motivated team. The second examines the processes you need to underpin and sustain your motivating environment, looking at setting objectives, measuring performance, and at how you reward people. The third teaches you the skills you need to develop in order to motivate your team. The final section looks at motivating in difficult situations such as dealing with change and motivating people who work from home.

Chapter 1

Creating a motivating environment

The context of motivation is important, as it is an essential element in the mix that delivers high performance. As a manager you will need to understand the principles of motivation to create the right environment in your organization.

Supporting performance

Motivation is a major driver of individual, team, and organizational success. But having motivated people isn't sufficient to guarantee high performance. There are other factors that must be considered, including having the ability and opportunity to do well.

TIP

MOTIVATE EVERYONE

In every team, some members demand more attention than others. Make sure you motivate all team members, even the quiet ones.

Directing efforts

Motivation is the will to do something. It comes from inside us, and herein lies the challenge for management: how do you motivate your people to achieve the organization's goals? Motivation is more than enthusiasm – it is about directing people's efforts. If you are a manager, your performance will depend on the efforts of your employees. Set clear goals for them and keep thinking about how you can support and motivate them. This is essential for the organization's and your own success.

Achieving success

A motivated person or group also requires the opportunity and ability to boost their performance. Opportunity covers two aspects – ensuring that your people have the tools and resources needed to do the job, and allowing them the space to do the job well without restrictions. A person's ability is a crucial factor that is often overlooked. It is created by combining an individual's innate skill or talent with experience.

Maximizing performance

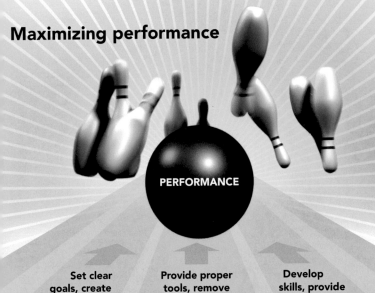

PERFORMANCE

Set clear goals, create enthusiasm

Provide proper tools, remove constraints

Develop skills, provide experience

MOTIVATION

OPPORTUNITY

ABILITY

Principles of motivation

There are three accepted theories of motivation: Maslow's hierarchy of needs, Herzberg's motivation and hygiene factors, and expectancy theory. How you use these, coupled with your own beliefs, will influence how you manage and motivate people.

GET FAMILIAR WITH YOUR STAFF
Remember everybody is an individual. To motivate someone you need to get to know them well and understand their own personal motivators and demotivators.

Maslow's motivation theory

American psychologist Abraham Maslow, one of the founding fathers of motivation theory, suggested that people have a hierarchy of needs. The basic needs should be satisfied first, and once these are met, you must appeal to the higher level of needs if you are to continue to motivate someone. Maslow's work suggests that people have different needs at different times. Some of these needs will be satisfied at work, and others through life outside work. But if you want to motivate your staff you need to get to know them, their interests, and their aspirations so you can adapt the organization's as well as your own approach to their changing situation.

IN FOCUS... MASLOW'S HIERARCHY OF NEEDS THEORY

Maslow's hierarchy of needs starts with the physiological needs of life: being able to breathe, being fed, and staying warm. The next level is concerned with security: being safe and secure. The third level relates to social needs: love and membership of wider social groups. The fourth level is esteem: the need for respect and a feeling of worth. The final level is self-actualization, where the desire is to be happy through achieving ambitions and fulfilling your potential. Maslow believed that once a lower level need was satisfied, its motivational impact declined and was replaced by higher level needs.

Expectancy theory

Expectancy theory was developed by Professor Victor Vroom in the 1960s. It proposes that people are motivated by being involved in setting their own goals, by receiving feedback along the way, and by recognition for what they achieve. Feedback is important, since it is very motivating to know how well you are progressing towards the target.

Herzberg's theory

The psychologist Frederick Herzberg divided sources of motivation into "motivators" and "hygiene factors". Hygiene factors don't motivate, but if they are not dealt with, they can turn people off. Having a dirty office is irritating, but having the cleanest office in the world isn't motivational. Herzberg believed salary is often a hygiene factor. If people are paid fairly, they are satisfied, but paying above the norm doesn't motivate people.

TIP

LOOK BEYOND SALARY

Focus on the other benefits you can use to motivate people including recognition, advancement, and development.

Herzberg's motivators and hygiene factors

HERZBERG'S HYGIENE FACTORS

HERZBERG'S MOTIVATORS

MOTIVATION

Salary	Recognition
Supervision	Progression
Company policy	Achievement
Working conditions	Responsibility
Personal relationships	The work itself

Believing in people

Your beliefs about human nature affect how you manage people. Douglas McGregor, author of *The Human Side of Enterprise*, created two extreme management approaches which he called theory X and theory Y. Theory X is based on the structuring of work precisely and at a detailed level, directing and controlling what people do, and motivating them through rewards and punishment. Theory Y suggests appealing to people's higher-level needs through communicating and negotiating goals and outcomes. If managers in your organization act as if they believe in theory X, employees are likely to be demotivated. You can set rules to protect the organization from lazy and uncommitted employees.

Theory X beliefs
• People are lazy.
• People lack ambition, dislike responsibility, and need to be told what to do.
• People are unconcerned by the organization's goals and need to be driven to perform.

Theory Y beliefs
• Most people are not naturally lazy, and work is a source of satisfaction.
• Most people learn to accept responsibility.
• Most people will work towards objectives to which they are committed.

GIVE CREDIT
Most people appreciate external recognition of their achievements so publicize their success and good work.

OFFER FEEDBACK
Keep talking and discussing with your staff – people need to receive regular feedback on progress in order to continue to perform well.

ALIGN GOALS
To achieve the organization's goals, translate them into goals that directly relate to each individual's job.

Directing motivation

SET TARGETS
People perform better when they have clear targets to achieve. Try and quantify what is to be achieved and by when.

ENGAGE PEOPLE
Involving people in setting targets improves motivation, creates commitment, and increases the chances of success.

Creating the right conditions

Broadly speaking, elements of motivation can be divided into two groups: tangible elements, such as the physical working environment, and intangible elements, such as status. Tangible elements are known as "hygiene factors", which are the basic work needs. Intangible elements are known as "motivators". Some, such as pay, straddle both groups; for example, money pays your bills, but higher pay rates can also be a form of recognition.

TIP

KEEP YOUR EARS OPEN

Pay attention to the general office chatter to find out what frustrates people.

Recognizing basic needs

Although it may seem odd, working in smart surroundings is not the greatest motivator. It is very pleasant and can signal a certain status, but it's not essential. The majority of people want to do a good job. They want to work to the best of their ability. It will almost certainly take them longer to do something if they don't have the proper tools to do it. Basic work needs in an average office to include:

• Good light and ventilation
• A comfortable temperature
• Sufficient desk space
• A comfortable chair
• Reliable equipment and systems such as a computer, printer, photocopier, and telephone
• An area for refreshment
• A separate area to get away from the desk.

TIP

BUILD A REPUTATION

Focus on establishing your organization's credibility – it can take years but will enable you to attract the best employees away from your competitors.

Considering intangible motivators

Intangible motivators are more difficult to identify and usually vary from person to person, although there are some that are common to most people. These fall across a spectrum ranging from those that are fairly easily defined, such as job security, flexible working, recognition, and career development, to those that are very personal, such as achievement – the feeling of having done a job well, belonging to a worthwhile organization, or being part of a well-respected team. These motivators are often highly prized and many people would rather work for an organization of which they are proud, or that takes account of their work-life balance, than for one that simply pays well.

✔ CHECKLIST ARE WORKING CONDITIONS OPTIMUM?

	YES	NO
• Is the physical working environment satisfactory?	☐	☐
• Are we offering a reasonable rate of pay?	☐	☐
• Does my team have the right tools for the job?	☐	☐
• Am I aware of what their frustrations are?	☐	☐
• Are we able to offer flexible working hours?	☐	☐
• Are our managers well trained?	☐	☐

Creating a high-performance culture

Some organizational cultures motivate people to perform well, while some motivate people to stay within their job description and not take risks. Your management style will create the culture for your team, so your actions are critical to motivation and performance.

Understanding culture

Blame culture — culture in which the organization looks to apportion blame rather than resolve problems. It is encapsulated by the question "whose fault is it?"

Culture is defined by an organization's values and behaviour. It is about the way things are done. Supportive cultures create a trusting environment that facilitates motivation. On the other hand, a blame culture* creates a climate of fear. Rather than promoting an environment in which mistakes are not made, it leads to one in which no one will take any risks and where people are more concerned about checking their own work than moving forward and achieving objectives.

CREATING A POSITIVE CULTURE

FAST TRACK	OFF TRACK
Demonstrating commitment to the organization's values	Lacking confidence in leaders
Focusing on opportunities	Covering up problems
Creating trust between people	Putting the blame on others
Learning from mistakes	Exercising too much control

Embedding the culture

TIP

BE PERSISTENT
To establish an open culture, always be asking "Why?" If you do not get the answer you need, keep asking until you reach the core of the issue.

A culture of openness motivates the whole team to perform. It is created by leaders communicating a clear vision of what they want the values of their organization to be. Many organizations publish their values and display them on their websites and intranet. The organization setting is important, but you should also create your own local team culture. To encourage a culture of openness you will need to respond positively when people present their mistakes or problems. You must use the opportunity to help people learn from their mistakes, rather than to pass judgement or criticize their actions. Believing that most people want to do a good job will help you do this. Over time, your action will create trust, and people will respond to your approach and confide in you. As you resolve their issues, you will motivate the whole team to perform.

Recruiting the right people

Most managers inherit existing teams and have the task of managing people with a given set of experience, skills, and personalities. When you bring in a new person, you can make a considerable difference to the performance and overall motivation of your team.

Introducing a new recruit

Long-established teams usually build good working relationships and have a strong sense of loyalty to the team and the organization, but they can also develop a reluctance to change and make improvements. Individuals may have become bored, and be demotivated as a result. Bringing in a person with new ideas can re-motivate a team. However, if you bring in the wrong person or handle their integration into the team ineptly, you may damage the team spirit. So it is important to consider a new recruit carefully.

Finding the right recruit

There are two key questions to ask when recruiting. The first is: "Does this person have the right experience, knowledge, and skill to do the job?" The second relates to attitude and approach: "How will this person contribute to the team and the organization?" The answers to the first question should be apparent from the individual's CV, and can be checked at the interview. The answers to the second can be sought during the interview process. Spotting self-motivated personnel is a challenging task. You can judge whether the individual is self-motivated by finding out whether they progressed in their previous organization, have learnt from mistakes, and if they have interests outside work.

Ensuring successful recruitment

Recruitment is an expensive process, so when you bring in a new person you want to make sure they stay and are successful in improving team performance. Your role as manager is to ensure that the new recruit has the best possible start. Consider how you will introduce them and integrate them into your existing team. Make sure team members are aware of the person's background and what they will be doing. Brief the individual on their personal objectives and the overall team objectives. If you work in a large organization you may want to appoint a mentor to work closely with the person through the early stages in their new role.

 ## IN FOCUS... DOCTOR BELBIN'S TEAM ROLES

Dr R. Meredith Belbin, a British researcher and management theorist, established a set of team roles, each associated with a particular type of personality. These included implementers, shapers, completer/finishers, plants (people who have original ideas), evaluators, specialists, co-ordinators, team workers, and resource investigators (people who explore new ideas). To succeed, teams need a balance of functional ability (the professional skills and technical backgrounds required for the project) and their team roles. Teams work best when there is a balance of roles so that the team members can motivate and learn from each other.

Measuring motivation

Motivation is not something you can easily sense when you walk into an office. You may spot tangible signs, but often they represent just a snapshot of what is happening at a given time. So it is helpful to try to measure the mood of the workforce. This is best done by means of a survey.

TIP

KEEP ASKING FOR FEEDBACK
Persevere with regular surveys, even if the results of the first one shock you. Over time and with attention, you can improve your results and the motivation of your staff.

Conducting a survey

It is generally accepted that motivated employees perform better, so it is important to establish how your employees are feeling as objectively as you can. The best way to get reliable and anonymous feedback about the mood of the workforce is through a regular staff opinion survey. Markus Buckingham and Curt Coffman, management consultants at the Gallup organization, developed a set of 12 questions to measure the motivation of a workforce. Does your staff:
• know what is expected of them at work?
• have the materials and equipment they need to do their job properly?
• have the opportunity to do their best every day?
• receive recognition or praise for good work? Have they in the last week?
• have a supervisor, or someone at work who cares about them as a person?
• have someone who encourages their development?
• believe their opinions at work appear to count?
• believe the mission of the company is important?
• believe their co-workers are committed to their work?
• have a best friend at work?
• have someone to talk to about their progress?
• have opportunities at work to learn and grow?

They also suggest you should ask how satisfied your employees are with your organization as an employer. Their research showed that responses to the questions can be positively linked to productivity, profitability, customer satisfaction, and staff turnover. Conducting the survey each year will allow you to compare the results over time, and reveal where improvements are being made and where you need to take action.

Providing feedback

If you conduct a survey, it is always important to give feedback. Ideally you should communicate this at team level, but when teams have returned fewer than seven completed surveys, you should not give the results, as anonymity will be undermined. Present and discuss the results openly, focusing on issues raised by the survey and actions that could be taken to avoid problems and improve things in the future. Be careful not to over-promise to avoid creating unrealistic expectations amongst your employees.

TIP

CHECK THE RESPONSE RATE

When conducting a survey, always measure your response rate – the number responding as a percentage of those sent the survey. A low response in an area can be an early indicator of problems.

MEASURING STAFF OPINION

FAST TRACK

OFF TRACK

FAST TRACK	OFF TRACK
Conducting regular staff opinion surveys	Disregarding or being uninterested in staff opinion
Allowing the staff to make their responses anonymous	Discouraging completion of the staff survey
Taking the survey seriously so that a majority of staff complete it	Asking the staff ambiguous or irrelevant questions

Chapter 2

Building processes for motivation

Once you have succeeded in creating an environment to develop a motivated workforce, you need to implement and maintain processes to underpin it. These processes provide a structure that demonstrates "how things are done".

Designing a job role

Jobs roles are changing as a result of the breaking down of hierarchy in organizations. Individuals now have a greater choice of what their job profile should be, so to retain the best employees and motivate them at work, you will need to design their job roles carefully.

TIP

BE ENTHUSIASTIC
Give full attention and energy to your own job role, only then will you be able to understand and design a suitable job role for your employees.

Making a job role motivational

You may work in a pleasant environment, but if you see no purpose in your job, you are unlikely to be motivated. This is why it is so important to design a job role that is suitable for each employee. In a well-designed job, the job-holder should be able to use a variety of skills in their job, be involved in the whole activity, and have a meaningful role in which they understand the impact of the work they do. You should give your staff freedom to carry out tasks and provide them with regular feedback on what they are doing well as well as where they need to improve.

Improving a job role

Few managers have the opportunity to design a job role from scratch. Unless you are embarking on a major change programme, any new job will almost certainly have to fit in with the current structure. However, you can make changes that will have a significant effect on motivation in your team. Every individual has different strengths and skills. If you understand what these are, you may be able to allocate the work in your team to play to someone's strengths. Bring your team together and ask them to think about their jobs and how they could be better designed. Be careful, though, because any changes have to be made in the light of the overall effectiveness of the organization. For example, deciding that you will unilaterally agree a policy of flexible working for your team is probably not a good idea for the organization as a whole. An effective way of improving existing jobs is job rotation – moving people around so that they develop a broader range of skills and gain experience of doing other jobs. Job enrichment is a means of giving people greater depth rather than breadth in their roles. It is about giving them more responsibility, autonomy, and discretion. This is often done to add interest where people are in very straightforward jobs.

TIP

ASSESS YOUR OWN ROLE

Think about your role. What do you like about it? What do you not like? Can you change it? Does it give you any pointers as to how your staff perceive their own roles?

ASK YOURSELF... HOW DO I DEFINE A ROLE?

- What is the tangible outcome of the role?
- What would happen if the role did not exist?
- What place does the role have in the structure of the organization?
- Do I know my employees well enough to design a suitable role for them?
- Could the role be broken down and shared amongst existing employees?
- Can I enrich the existing job role?
- How will the results of the post-holder's contribution be measured?

Creating a balance

In motivating people to perform well, you should aim to balance high performance with constructive behaviour as well as balance short-term success with achieving longer-term goals. It is also important to give equal weight to the needs of the organization and the individual.

Balancing performance indicators and behaviour

*Gaming — *the behaviour associated with achieving the target numbers by any means and without regard for delivering real performance.*

Most measurements of performance don't give a view of the future. Take the sales target as an example. Close to the month end, a salesman may make unrealistic promises to his customers and take orders that will allow him to reach his bonus. This will ensure achievement of the performance target, but his behaviour may upset the customer in the longer term, causing his customer to place their business elsewhere. This behaviour is gaming* the system and as a manager you need to take steps to avoid this.

Balancing short- and long-term needs

TIP

CHOOSE YOUR STYLE

In a crisis, short-term motivational techniques will be most appropriate, but make sure you return to long-term techniques when the crisis is over.

Motivation has short- and long-term elements. In the short term, commitment, direction, and enthusiasm will motivate people. But in the longer term, people need to see that they are being led and that changes are being made to help them do their work. In the longer term, giving people the right tools, creating the right working environment, and giving them the training they need is much more motivational. Short-term success has to be translated into long-term success by changing the way the work is done.

Blake–Mouton management grid

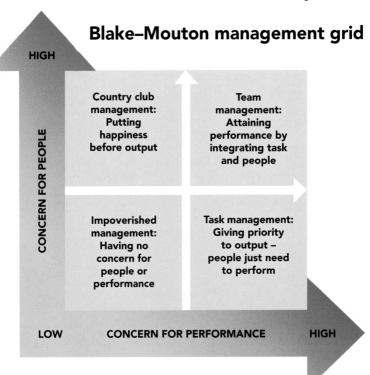

HIGH

CONCERN FOR PEOPLE

Country club management: Putting happiness before output

Team management: Attaining performance by integrating task and people

Impoverished management: Having no concern for people or performance

Task management: Giving priority to output – people just need to perform

LOW   CONCERN FOR PERFORMANCE   HIGH

Balancing work and individual needs

Ask yourself whether you are people-focused or task-focused – do you devote most of your effort to achieving the goals that have been set for the organization, or do you focus on ensuring that people are content in their jobs? In reality, you should do both. The organization needs to achieve its goals and targets, so these are important.

However, the people who work for the organization have their own needs and these can't be ignored. The key to motivational management is to align your employees' needs closely with those of the organization. Management theorists Robert Blake and Jane Mouton created a grid that reflects four approaches to management. They suggest that managers should aim to be in the top right hand box, showing high concern for both people and performance.

Conducting appraisals

An appraisal is a formal process for setting objectives, measuring progress, and providing feedback to employees on performance. When conducted in an appropriate manner, it can motivate individuals to perform more effectively and progress within the organization.

Benefiting from appraisals

One of the key benefits of the appraisal process is that it provides a structured approach to managing performance. This is important, as personal objectives are essential to guiding motivation. It also forces managers to sit down and have a frank discussion with each team member. It is important not to rely on the appraisals alone to manage your team; you will need to monitor performance regularly and communicate informally as well. However, having an organization-wide mechanism for managing performance and career aspirations is invaluable.

REVIEWING
Assess the individual's performance and discuss their career aspirations.

Focusing on the "how"

Appraisals normally consist of formal meetings between the individual and their immediate manager, focusing on objectives and their progress. Discuss how the objective is being achieved as well as what has been achieved. The "how" is essential for long-term success. If an individual has achieved a high level of output but has poached resources from other teams to achieve this, take this into account while assessing performance.

RECORD KEEPING
Take down detailed notes of issues discussed and action points for the future.

Elements of an appraisal

GOAL SETTING
Review progress against current objectives and set new objectives that are linked to the organization's goals.

ANALYSIS
Consider development needs for the current role and future progression if appropriate.

EXAMINATION
Talk about more intangible issues, such as how objectives have been achieved.

COMMUNICATION
Discuss specific problems, especially those that have prevented your employee from meeting an objective.

Setting objectives

Setting objectives is one of the most difficult tasks a manager faces. If the objectives are too hard, people can become demotivated, but if they are too easy, people coast along. Objective setting takes time and effort, but it is the only real way of directing your staff.

TIP

EVALUATE THE OBJECTIVES
There is a saying "what gets measured gets done", so ensure the goals you set correspond with what you want the individual to deliver.

Setting objectives in context

Everybody in your organization is dependent on the efforts of other people, so, in setting objectives, you need to take account of the context. For example, the sales team is often seen as a department where targets are achieved solely through the efforts of the sales people, but this is not the case. The team that processes the orders is also important, as are those who designed and created a good product. Motivating people to exert higher levels of effort will improve performance, but in many administrative, service, and manufacturing jobs the system has a much greater impact on the level of output than the effort of individual employees. As a manager you will need to keep this in mind while setting goals for your employees to avoid unrealistic expectations from your staff.

Linking objectives to strategy

TIP

SET RELEVANT GOALS
Ensure that you don't set objectives just because they are easily measurable. Always think: does this objective really matter?

People are motivated when their objectives are linked to the overall goals of the organization and they can see how they contribute to the organization's success. Without this line of sight, people can easily lose their sense of purpose at work, which can adversely affect their motivation. Cascade the objectives down through the organization, with each department having a stated aim and a set of goals that must be reached to achieve the overall objective.

Achieving objectives through targets

Break down objectives into individual targets that can be used as measures of performance. For example, the objective might be to improve the quality of customer service in a restaurant, and the targets following from that might be to have all diners seated within five minutes of their arrival, to have orders transmitted to the kitchen within five minutes of being taken, and to clear tables within five minutes of the diners vacating them.

Creating stretch goals

Stretch goals are goals that are demanding, but not impossible to reach – often described as "high but achievable". You will need to be careful when you set these goals to make them work. Here are some tips to help you avoid the pitfalls:
• Understanding past performance will be important – you should know what your employee is capable of if you want to set a stretch goal. Your employee may well be looking to set an easier target, so there is a limit to how much you can rely on their input.
• Targets are usually set in advance for the year, but circumstances can change rapidly in a volatile environment. To keep your people focused and motivated, be prepared to be flexible and reset the targets to maintain the stretch.
• Targets need to be seen as being fair. The degree of difficulty should be the same for all. Often, the targets you set across your team will vary from individual to individual, according to the requirements of the task and the team's overall capabilities. Explain carefully why the targets have been set. If they are perceived as being unequal, they will cause friction and demotivation.

HOW TO... SET TARGETS

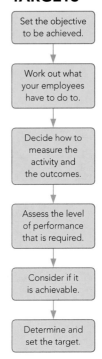

Set the objective to be achieved.

Work out what your employees have to do to.

Decide how to measure the activity and the outcomes.

Assess the level of performance that is required.

Consider if it is achievable.

Determine and set the target.

TIP

EQUIP YOUR STAFF
Consider what people need to do their job. It is frustrating if you can't perform because of lack of equipment.

Creating personal objectives

Not all the objectives you set should be linked to short-term performance outcomes. There must be a balance between the needs of the organization and those of the individual. Training and development may take your staff away from their day-to-day job and may require the organization to spend money, but setting a personal development goal is motivational as it demonstrates the organization is interested in the individual and their long-term career. As part of the appraisal process, discuss the employees' skills and longer term development needs and include these in their personal objectives.

TIP

PULL TOGETHER
Allocate a shared objective to multiple people. The benefits of working as a team outweigh the motivation of individual objectives.

Communicating the objectives

How you set objectives is very important. Set targets face to face with your employees. This will allow you to explain what the targets are and discuss their feasibility and implications. To be motivational, objectives need to be owned, so discuss them with your employees to get feedback. This will help you gauge whether they are prepared to accept the objective. Choose a suitable channel to communicate with them. If you distribute the sales targets for the year by e-mail, it will tell everyone what is required, but does little for motivation. If you manage too many people to see them all individually, consider how to reorganize the reporting relationship to ensure each individual is managed properly.

Defining a S.U.S.T.A.I.N.A.B.L.E objective

STRETCHING
It requires commitment and effort

UNDERSTOOD
Employees know what has to be achieved, what is required, and why it is important

SUPPORTED
It includes a plan of action that should ensure success

TIME BOUND
Everyone knows what has to be achieved by when

ACHIEVABLE
It is realistic within resource and time constraints

INCLUSIVE
It draws colleagues into achieving the goal

NEGOTIATED
Objectives are agreed upon rather than imposed

ANSWERABLE
Performance outcome, not the activity, is measured

BELIEVED
It is seen as the right objective to be achieved

LINKED
It is consistent with the organization's goals

EXPLAINED
It is clearly stated with measurable outcomes

Measuring progress

Feedback is an important element of motivation. Once objectives have been set it is important that you track and monitor progress and discuss it with your staff. But you also need to know when to intervene and when to leave a situation alone.

Measuring key activities

*KPI — "Key Performance Indicator". KPIs track performance of the organization against its higher-level goals.

The usual way of measuring progress is to plot a graph of KPIs*, such as monthly sales figures, against the target. But not all progress can be tracked so simply – some projects require considerable input before change in the output can be measured. To avoid demotivating your staff, you need to measure progress against each of the activities that contributes to achieving the outcome.

Feeding back results

Measurement provides feedback and feedback should be acted upon. For the measurement to be motivational, make sure that those being measured see the results and understand how they were calculated. If this doesn't happen, they will not know how to improve their performance. Ideally, people need to measure their own performance, so that feedback is instantaneous. This way the individual or team can see quickly how they are progressing, allowing them to act even before management is alerted to a problem – for example, keeping a graph of calls handled or components produced provides feedback in real time. But you can't measure progress on all aspects of your work. Sometimes others have to measure your work for you – many accounting measures fall into this category.

TIP

REGULATE

Measure often, but be aware that if you measure too often, you may not be able to detect any change.

Choosing the right measure

You need to choose the correct indicator to measure your employees' performance. For instance, how would you assess the performance of a maintenance team? Is it good if they are constantly busy and working long hours? Does this show how motivated they are? If they are all sitting down drinking coffee is it because they are lazy and demotivated? In fact, you want your maintenance team to be idle most of the time, as this means that all the equipment is working and your factory is producing. Be careful to choose the correct measure, and not to confuse high levels of activity with performance.

ASK YOURSELF... AM I MEASURING CORRECTLY?

- Do I have a clear measure of performance?
- Do I have a clear measure of activity?
- Do I know how much effort is required to perform well?
- Do I review performance regularly?
- Do I give feedback regularly?
- Do I use the measures of performance in formal reviews?
- Do I use the measures to take decisions?
- Do I communicate performance indicators to all those involved?
- Do I ensure that all those involved understand what the performance is and how we deliver it?
- Do I understand the external factors that affect the performance being measured?

CASE STUDY

"Andon" way of measuring

Many Japanese car manufacturers use an "Andon" system on their production lines. This system allows a worker to stop the whole production line because he has encountered a problem he can't solve himself. When this process was adopted in a European car plant, the flashing lights triggered by the Andon system brought all the managers down onto the shop floor. They would remain there to provide support and motivation until the plant restarted. As problems reduced and the Andon system was used less frequently, managers stayed away. Though this was a sign of success, the production workers didn't see it as such as they lost touch with their managers making them feel neglected and less inclined to use the system when things went wrong. The company eventually realized their mistake and ensured that management discussed and reviewed progress with the production workers regularly and, most importantly, celebrated success together.

Training and development

Research has shown that employees, particularly young people, value development opportunities. A company that offers training and development is showing commitment to its employees, developing them for the future, and helping them to do a better job in the process.

TIP

MATCH TRAINING WITH ABILITY
Some people prefer to learn by "doing" and others are happy to read about a subject or listen to a lecture, so consider what you want the training to achieve, and then establish how the individual learns best.

Making the case for training

Training should be encouraged so that it is woven into the culture of the organization. Having a good training scheme and being aware of development needs are good ways of attracting the best people to join your organization, of motivating them, and also of retaining them. This can give a business a substantial advantage over its competitors. It is essential that the training itself is of a good standard, otherwise it is a waste of time. Though the appraisal meeting provides a formal opportunity for the individual and manager to discuss training, development needs arise throughout the year and should be addressed from time to time to ensure success. You must also ensure the training meets the employee's own development needs to keep them motivated.

Getting the best from training

Any type of training involves spending time or money (and usually both), so it is important to ensure you derive maximum benefit from it. Make sure you seek out underlying needs, suited to the individual's job role. For example, if they are learning a skill, make sure they will be able to practise it. Having established these, you should brief the individual beforehand on what they can expect from the training. Discuss afterwards what they have learnt and how they should use it.

SUPPORT
Help staff to make and handle changes in their current job.

Facilitating development

MOULD
Prepare your employees for their next roles in the organization.

IMPROVE
Help your staff to work better and smarter in their current jobs.

ENHANCE
Encourage staff to aquire further professional qualifications.

Exploring ways of development

Rather than sending employees for external training, you can consider other methods of development:
- **Job rotation** Moving around the organization to learn different jobs and acquire new skills and knowledge in the process.
- **Secondment** Working in another department on a project, to give a broader perspective to their work.
- **Coaching and mentoring** Receiving one-to-one support from a more experienced colleague.
- **Professional qualification** A qualification in marketing or finance can provide a life-time benefit. This requires a lot of of time and effort, so both the individual and the organization must be ready to commit.

MANAGE EXPECTATIONS

Increase your employees' prospects in the organization after they complete the training by offering them more responsibility, or they might look for a better opportunity somewhere else.

Recognizing performance

Most people think money is the key motivator and reward for good performance. It isn't. It may be motivating to have a pay rise or bonus but the effects are often short-lived. Simple recognition is a very powerful motivator, and can and should occur every day. Just praising someone who is doing something well can make all the difference, and costs nothing.

USE INGENIOUS WAYS TO PRAISE

Make praise public. For example, print out customer commendations and place them on the notice board for everyone to see.

Giving recognition

Everyone likes to receive a thank you and to get credit for work well done. Identifying when things have been done well and recognizing this formally is an excellent way of motivating on a day-to-day basis.

All organizations should ensure that the basics of recognition, such as saying "thank you", are ingrained in all employees. However, many companies also run formal recognition systems. These tend to reward the teams or individuals with the greatest output, those who have built good relationships with their customers, and those who have supported their colleagues most.

Recognition, whether formal or informal, is a way of ensuring that people, and managers in particular, are on the lookout for good performance, and promote it around the company. Here are some other ways to recognize the efforts of your employees:

• Send them an e-mail thanking them for their support.
• Copy their boss into the thank-you e-mail.
• Take them (or the team) out for a drink after work.
• Buy them and their partner dinner.
• Give them a bunch of flowers or a box of chocolates with a note.
• Explain at the team meeting what they did and why it was so good.
• Create a scheme for "employee of the month".
• Give them a half-day holiday.
• Ensure that your team celebrates success.

Using the personal touch

Informal recognition systems may rely on local management initiative, but they are essential. They require managers to know what is going on and to be able to spot good work and high levels of effort. As a manager, you need to be involved in what your employees are doing and saying. This, in itself, is motivating to your staff, who see that you are interested in their work.

However, be aware that recognition is not as simple as saying "thank you" – people can see when you aren't being sincere. It is important to react spontaneously when you notice their efforts and mean what you say. Tell your boss about employees who perform well – being perceived positively by the senior management will boost their morale. Your staff will also appreciate it if you make a personal effort to recognize good performance by thanking them face-to-face. If appropriate, consider an inexpensive gift such as flowers or chocolates, although if you start doing this, make it a policy for all high-performing employees, to avoid accusations of favouritism.

✔ CHECKLIST **RECOGNIZING WORK**

	YES	NO
• Do you always say thank you?	☐	☐
• Do you always make a positive comment when work is done well?	☐	☐
• Do you try to catch your staff doing something well every week?	☐	☐
• When you see exceptional performance, do you tell everyone?	☐	☐
• Do you buy a small gift to say thank you when appropriate?	☐	☐
• Do you exploit the formal recognition system for good performance?	☐	☐

Paying for performance

Pay is often used as a motivator. It can take the form of salary increases, commission, or bonuses. Rules can be set in advance for deciding how much is paid using a particular formula, or a judgement can be made at the end of the year as to how much is deserved.

TIP

STAY ON TRACK

Always link bonuses back to what the organization is trying to achieve in the long run. If you don't, you will be rewarding behaviour that is not benefiting the organization.

Motivating through pay

The motivational element of pay comes from linking the level of financial return to the performance of an individual or team. The intention is to motivate people to put in more effort because they know they will receive a greater financial reward. Here are some other reasons for linking pay and performance:
• To follow the norm in the industry
• To manage costs – pay is given in proportion to the financial results received.

Linking pay and performance

To link pay and performance, you must be able to objectively measure the element of performance you wish to reward. You need to select the elements you reward with care – if you reward only one element of performance you will need other management approaches to ensure other aspects are not neglected. Fairness is one of the most important factors in linking performance with reward. When the system is seen to be fair, people will be motivated. If people work independently, then reward the individual for his or her performance. If team effort is required, you must reward the team effort. Target setting is the most difficult aspect of linking pay to performance. You will need to collect enough data to be sure that your target is both stretching and attainable.

METHODS OF LINKING PAY AND PERFORMANCE

METHOD	POSITIVE IMPACT	NEGATIVE IMPACT
Directly linking bonus to achieving specific targets	• Makes the reward mechanism very clear • Encourages very specific behaviour	• Can become very rigid and therefore irrelevant if circumstances at the workplace change
Indirectly linking bonus and pay to performance	• Allows managers to exercise their judgement • Allows a more rounded view of performance	• Makes the reward mechanism less clear
Setting targets through consultation	• Motivates people through engagement in the target-setting process	• Can become a negotiation • Will encourage people to set easy targets • Will encourage people to hoard (rather than share) information
Linking size of incentive to goals	• Large incentives will be acted on • Small incentives help communication of goals	• Large incentives may encourage cheating • Small incentives may fail to motivate people
Paying a bonus when a fixed-value target is achieved	• The threshold target becomes specific and is easy to comprehend	• There is no incentive to perform once the target is reached • There is no incentive to perform if the target becomes unattainable • Encourages gaming – the pulling forward and putting back of performance between periods to achieve the bonus
Paying a bonus at each step towards achieving a target	• Creates an incentive to perform over a range of outcomes • Rewards high performers for their work	• Sets a less specific expectation
Linking performance to salary increases	• Reduces costs as increments are usually smaller than bonus payments	• Invariably, such increases are paid for the rest of the employee's time of service
Setting targets afterwards by comparison with others	• Makes targets appropriate in nearly all circumstances	• Makes the link between effort and performance, and performance and reward, less clear

Chapter 3

Developing the skills of motivation

Once you have learnt the principles of motivation and how to create the right environment for it to flourish, you need to develop the skills to motivate your team. It is important to practise these skills continually to increase your capability.

Motivating yourself

As a manager, you are a role model: your staff will notice what you say, how you say it, and how you behave. It is important that you are motivated yourself. Remember that the principles of motivation apply just as much to you as they do to your team.

Understanding what you want

BE PROACTIVE
If you don't like something and you can change it or think it can be changed, take positive action.

It is worth thinking about what you really want. This will help to motivate you and enable you to structure your ambitions and goals. Understanding what you want applies to your personal life as much as to your work life – the two are intertwined. If you really want to spend more time with your family then you are unlikely to be motivated if you are in a job where you are required to spend many hours at work. If you come to the conclusion that you're not in the right job, you are better off moving to a new job that suits your circumstances better.

Knowing what motivates you

Most people are so busy with their day-to-day activities that they don't take time out to reflect on what they enjoy doing. Everyone has to do tasks they don't like, but if you can build several tasks you really enjoy into your day, it will help to keep you motivated. Think about your work – what aspects do you enjoy? Is it contact with people? Writing a report? Creating a new idea? Can you do more of these activities? What do you not enjoy? Can you minimize the time you spend on these tasks in future? Is there a better way of doing them? It is easy to put off tasks you don't enjoy doing, but this is a mistake because the thought of doing them remains on your mind. The trick is to do them, get them out of the way, and start something you really want to do that will motivate you.

Setting your own goals

Set goals for yourself, just as you would for your staff. This gives you something to aim for. Ensure your goals mean something to you, to give you a sense of achievement. Be precise and set a timeframe, so that you can monitor your progress. If the goal is large, break it down into manageable chunks. Don't say "I will increase my personal network of contacts"; say instead, "I will add five new contacts to my personal network from the construction sector by the end of December."

Goals don't have to be totally work-related. In fact, it is a good idea to have some personal goals. For example, you might decide that you need to lose weight or improve your health. In this case one of your goals might be to lose 5kg (11lb) or to participate in some organized runs by a certain date.

To give yourself some extra motivation to achieve your chosen goals, spend some time visualizing what it will be like when you have achieved them.

Dealing with problems

From time to time, problems will arise at work. They generally fall into two groups: those you can ease or solve and those you can do nothing about. It is no use worrying about something you cannot change. Recognize this, work around it, and get on as best as you can without brooding. If the problem is beyond your control but is very important to you, speak to your boss. If possible, come up with a solution yourself and suggest it to them.

Learning from mistakes

It is easy to lose motivation when you have made a mistake, but remember that no one is perfect. If you aren't making any mistakes, it probably means you aren't taking any risks and are staying within your "comfort zone". If a mistake occurs, do not make excuses or blame someone else. Accept constructive criticism, learn what you can from it, and move on.

DEALING WITH CRITICISM

FAST TRACK

OFF TRACK

FAST TRACK	OFF TRACK
Listening to what is being said	Becoming defensive
Making sure you understand what you are being criticized for	Focusing on failure
Seeking clarification if necessary	Taking it personally
Reflecting on the action to take	Dwelling on past problems

Being positive

If all you do is moan about problems and always appear negative, you will have no hope of motivating your staff. But this does not mean you always have to be cheerful and only see the advantages in everything around you. It is important to be realistic. If you have started a project and you can see problems with it, your first task is to find ways of resolving them. If the problems really can't be resolved, you will probably have to work around them. Let your staff know what the problems are, but also tell them that you will help to work through them. Ensure they know what your expectations are of them.

Balancing work and life

Successful people usually have a wide range of hobbies and interests outside work, together with a broad network of friends and contacts. It is often helpful to share problems with people away from your place of work because they see them in a new light. Even if you thoroughly enjoy your job, do not become a workaholic. If you spend all your time concentrating on your work you will eventually become tired, dissatisfied, and demotivated.

Being a good motivator

Motivation is not just about understanding and applying the theories – it is about how you put them into practice. In essence, being a good motivator is part of being a good leader – someone who people follow. For this to happen, you need the personal characteristics that make people want to follow you.

TIP

BE AWARE
Pay attention to what is going on around you to understand what motivates your staff, but ensure you don't get involved in gossip.

Knowing what makes a good motivator

There is no single "good" management style that will turn you into a good motivator. If you try to adopt a style with which you feel uncomfortable, you will come across as being insincere and you won't be trusted. However, there are some characteristics that all good motivators share. It is worth reflecting on the people you believe are good motivators – what was it about them that spurred you on to achieve? This will give you an insight into your own personal motivation, as well as helping you to consider how you can motivate your team.

✔ CHECKLIST ARE YOU A GOOD MOTIVATOR?

	YES	NO
• Can you be trusted – do what you say you will do?	☐	☐
• Can you build rapport with individuals on the team?	☐	☐
• Are you loyal to your team?	☐	☐
• Are you fair in your dealings with people?	☐	☐
• Do you share credit with the team for achievements?	☐	☐
• Can you see the individual's perspective whilst keeping the organization's goal in mind?	☐	☐

Balancing trust and authority

One of the most important characteristics of good motivators is that they can be trusted. It is only possible to motivate people for a very short time without gaining their trust. To gain the trust of your team, never make promises you can't keep – if you let people down, they will be very wary in the future. If something goes wrong, it is your job as the leader of the team to take responsibility and criticism for it. You have to defend your team in public while investigating in private what went wrong and how it can be avoided in the future. As a manager, you have a difficult balance to strike between "being one of the team" and being the leader. Quite where this balance will lie will depend on the structure and culture of the organization. Some have very "flat" structures where there is very little difference between managers and their staff – others have more hierarchy. Whatever the culture in your organization, some distance should be maintained, or your own authority can be undermined, making it difficult for you to manage problems with poor performers. If there is too much distance, however, you will never get to know the individuals in your team, and they won't know whether they can trust you or not.

Focusing on the future

As a manager, you need to organize and take care of detail, but someone who spends all their time on this without seeing the wider context is unlikely to be a good motivator. You need to know how reaching your immediate goal will lead to achieving the ultimate objective. An often-quoted example of this is two bricklayers who are asked what they are doing. "I'm laying bricks," says one. The other says "I'm building a cathedral." A good motivator will paint a picture of the objective to strengthen their team's sense of purpose.

TIP

EMPATHIZE WITH YOUR STAFF

Understanding your team's problems and empathizing with their position will help you to motivate them better.

HOW TO... MOTIVATE YOUR STAFF

Share the vision with your team.

↓

Make the goals real to your people.

↓

Give regular feedback to your staff.

↓

Recognize performance.

↓

Celebrate success with all those involved.

Making people feel valued

If people feel valued by their manager, they will be prepared to make the extra effort that can make the difference between success and failure. However, in facing the day-to-day pressures of meeting deadlines and trying to achieve targets, many managers overlook the relatively small actions that show they value the individuals in their team.

Understanding the benefits

New employees are usually brimming with enthusiasm when they join an organization or begin a new role. But somewhere along the line, it is common for most staff to suffer from demotivation. If the organization fails to value its staff, why should they contribute whole-heartedly to the organization's success? Although "valuing someone" may sound intangible and woolly, research shows that employees who are valued perform better in their job and this, in turn, leads to higher levels of business performance.

REWARD
Not every organization can pay the best wages in the industry but it is important that your staff are rewarded fairly for their work and that they understand the organization's policy and see that it is applied consistently.

 IN FOCUS... COMMITMENT-BASED HR

Researchers have defined two types of HR practice: commitment based and transaction based. Commitment-based practices focus on developing the long-term relationship between the employer and the employee in an organization. Mentoring, training, and development are all examples of commitment-based practices.

Transaction-based practices focus on the here and now, just paying people for the work they do. A recent study in the UK showed that commitment-based practices increased employee engagement, which led to higher levels of product and service quality, innovation, and better financial performance.

RECOGNITION
Simply saying thank you when people are doing things well and taking the trouble to show that you appreciate them form the first step in valuing people.

PERSONAL TOUCH
Getting to know people as individuals so they feel you are taking an interest in them personally is vitally important. But make sure you extend the same level of interest and flexibility to all members of your team. It is easy to slip into the habit of favouritism.

Techniques for making staff feel valued

POWER OF EXPRESSION
Employees feel valued if their opinions are heard and taken into account during decision making.

TRAINING AND DEVELOPMENT
People feel valued if the organization invests in them and in their future. Organizations that invest in people find that people commit to them, so training and development become essential.

PROMOTION
People who perform well will look to progress in their career. Helping them in that progression demonstrates your commitment to them.

Developing communication

Communication and openness are important tools for motivation. If you don't communicate effectively, people will feel unimportant and undervalued. Ambiguous communication can also lead to the spreading of rumours, which is particularly unhealthy as they play on people's fears.

Sharing information

There is a balance between sharing what you know and worrying people unnecessarily. In some cases it is important first to consider the consequences of sharing information. Unless you are at the stage of consulting people, it is sometimes better to wait until you have some tangible ideas to put forward. Putting forward woolly thoughts rarely leads to people feeling they are being kept informed. They are more likely to think you are hiding something. However, it is better to err on the side of over-communicating than to hold information back.

Communicating well

Communication is a two-way process. It is not just about telling people something – it is also about listening to what is being said. Good motivators are people who think about what they are saying and how they are saying it. They constantly gauge the response from their listeners, and when they have spoken, they keep quiet and listen. In this way they gain insights into how people are feeling and receive new ideas and perspectives. Practise listening: you will be surprised by how much you can learn.

TIP

BE A GOOD LISTENER

Look at the speaker, lean forward, and encourage them by nodding your head. Good listeners will also ask questions and seek clarification if they do not understand a point.

Selecting the right channel

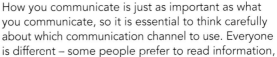

How you communicate is just as important as what you communicate, so it is essential to think carefully about which communication channel to use. Everyone is different – some people prefer to read information, others to hear it. If you have something important to say it is a good idea to use several different communication channels to strengthen your message and to appeal to people in different ways. Having a one-to-one meeting is good for dealing with individual problems but can be time consuming, while a team meeting allows discussion of issues and facilitates mutual understanding. The telephone is a convenient way to give information that is easy to understand. E-mails, newsletters, and the intranet are impersonal but provide an instant means of reaching a large number of people.

Managing politics

Politics in the workplace are hard to avoid. Whatever you do, cliques will form, people will jockey for position, and rumours will be spread. In the longer term this leads to energy being diverted away from the business and can even lead to victimization and bullying of individuals. It is important you know what is going on and put a stop to it. Politics can undermine the positive culture of the organization, and damage motivation. Bullying has the same effect, so when you detect this happening, act quickly and prevent it from happening in the future. Plug yourself into your organization's networks so you understand what is going on, but avoid letting it distract you from your own work.

Identifying demotivation

Demotivation in the workplace has a wide variety of causes, from tiredness and overwork to problems at home. Demotivated employees can affect the morale of their colleagues, and whole teams can also become demotivated, so it is essential to be able to spot the signs of demotivation and to act quickly.

Spotting the signs

Everyone has days when they feel demotivated and below par. Demotivation may not always be immediately apparent but there are some signs to watch out for. An employee may be slumped at their desk, gazing into space, or tapping their fingers on the desk. You can also tell how they are feeling from the tone of their voice. A monotonous tone or yawning may be signals that someone is bored or tired. While these are not always signs of serious demotivation and you shouldn't be too quick to jump to conclusions, you should still check them out. Other signs of demotivation include people who normally react well to requests failing to respond or avoiding volunteering for new tasks. Don't let too much time pass before you act. Anyone can have an off day, but if it persists, or there is a regular pattern to their mood swings, then you should talk to the individual concerned. If they feel overworked, see if you can re-allocate some of their work. Saying you appreciate what they have been doing can be enough to raise their spirits and re-motivate them. Even a quick "How are things today?" shows you have noticed and care about how they are feeling.

Dealing with performance issues

One of the most noticeable signs of more serious problems is when someone who is normally a good worker fails to perform. Of course, this may just be a one-off instance. Perhaps the individual has had a particularly difficult task to do or a difficult customer to deal with. But if their work is constantly below their normal standard, there is a problem that you need to tackle. Neither will this type of problem be solved by a quick question about how the person is, nor will it be solved by a military-style inquisition. You will need an in-depth discussion to identify what is wrong and what can be done to put it right. Discuss the problem in a confidential meeting, set targets for improving performance, and agree on a strategy to resolve it.

TIP

ACT QUICKLY

If you spot the signs of demotivation in one of your employees, their colleagues will see them too. Don't ignore the signs: take action quickly before the team think you haven't noticed or don't care.

Countering absenteeism

High levels of staff absenteeism are a strong sign of a demotivated team. To deal with this, talk to staff after every absence. Meet with every absent staff member, so that you cannot be accused of singling anyone out, but make the discussion private, so you can adapt your approach depending on how often the individual is absent and the underlying cause. The objective of the meeting is twofold: first, so your staff are aware that you have noted their absence, and second, to ascertain the cause. Finding out why people are absent is the first step to tackling the problem.

Be aware of staff turnover. Even if the figure for your department is below average, make sure you know why people are leaving. New staff bring in new ideas, but high levels of staff turnover unsettle a team and can demotivate those left behind. Your organizations' human resources team should always conduct exit interviews to establish why someone is leaving, and you must ensure the feedback is passed on to you.

Consulting others

Consultation plays an important part in motivation. Jointly setting goals and targets with others communicates what is to be achieved and increases their commitment to achieving them. So consult when you can, but realize that if you have to make a quick decision it is not always possible.

OPEN IT UP

Involve people in decision making whenever you can. Teams often make better decisions than individuals.

Involving people

Think about how you feel when you are told about decisions that directly affect you at work. How would you feel if they were announced with no prior warning or consultation? Sometimes it can be a pleasant surprise, but often you feel bewildered: "Why did they do that? What a stupid decision!" Now think about the decision on which you have been consulted or involved. You know why the decision was taken, and although you may not fully agree with it, you won't think it is stupid. Consulting avoids the immediate negative impact on morale and performance.

BE CLEAR

People need to know when you are giving orders and when you are consulting. Make this absolutely clear or you will cause confusion.

Benefiting from consultation

You will benefit from consulting with others because:
• You can involve others in the process of setting goals and agreeing on actions, drawing them into the process and increasing their commitment to the project.
• You will gain information from other persepectives, on the basis of which you can decide and act.
• You and your team will improve your understanding of what has to be achieved, and why.
• It can help you in setting targets at the right level.
• The whole process can be motivational and help to strengthen bonds within your teams.
• The final agreement strengthens the commitment of the team, ensuring they will perform.

KNOWING WHEN TO CONSULT

CONSULT...	DON'T CONSULT...
• When you have the time to consult.	• When people are expecting to be told what to do.
• When there is still time to influence the decision.	• When decisive action needs to be made quickly.
• When your team's input will improve the decision.	• When the decision has already been made.
• When you need the team to agree on the project's goal for its success.	• When there is an obvious technical expert whose advice you should follow.

Avoiding pitfalls

There are a number of pitfalls of consulting. It is important that people know when they are being consulted and when they are being informed of a decision. Some targets are not negotiable – they have been set high up in the company and allocated to your team. If you are going to consult in this situation you will need to explain that the target is not for negotiation, but you want input on how it is going to be met. Ask yourself whether the consultation is genuine and not a public-relations exercise. If there is little likelihood of the organization taking account of what is being discussed, you must still take feedback from your staff for them to let off steam, but also explain to them that while you will pass their comments on, you don't expect things to change as a result.

CASE STUDY

You don't know what you don't know

An electricity distribution company faced the issue of needing to undertake maintenance on its power lines but having to compensate customers every time the power was cut off. Staff worked quickly on the repairs, but the costs were high. In order to cascade the strategy down the organization, the objective of reducing the cost was delegated to the front-line maintenance team. They came up with the solution of buying a generator so the electric supply could be maintained whilst the repairs were made. When this was proposed to the finance director, his immediate reply was "Do you know what a generator costs?" They didn't, but he didn't know the cost of cutting the supply. The new generator cost $1 million, but by consulting the front-line staff and involving them in the decision-making process, the company rapidly paid off the cost of the generator and made significant savings.

Delegating effectively

Delegating tasks is not only a way to reduce your workload, it can also motivate employees. However, while having a task delegated to you can be a highly motivating experience, it can also result in loss of confidence and demotivation if you are unable to complete the tasks.

Knowing when to delegate

While delegation reduces your workload, it also means letting go of the task and giving it to someone else. This means you should only delegate tasks with a clear structure. Implement a monitoring process so that you can assure yourself that progress is being made and the person is comfortable with the task in hand. Delegate when the task is likely to be repeated, making it worth the time and effort, or when the task itself may be motivating for someone else to do. Avoid delegating if there are time constraints or the individual does not have the skill or experience.

5
SUPPORT
Encourage and guide
the individual
or team, give
feedback regularly,
and keep a check
on progress.

Deciding how to delegate

How to delegate will depend on the working environment, how well you know the person you are delegating to, their level of experience, and the importance of the task. Delegation takes time to do well. With an experienced team, it can be done over a cup of coffee, but if you have a critical project or you are working with people you don't know well, it is better to be formal. Ideally this should involve a face-to-face meeting supported by an e-mail or document recording what has been agreed. Ensure that you have allocated the time both to hand over the task and to follow up.

Delegating efficiently

1
IDENTIFY
Define the task, check that all the required resources are available, and specify the desired outcomes.

2
DISTRIBUTE
Decide who you are going to assign the task to and allocate the resources in a judicious manner.

3
BRIEF
Communicate and agree the goals with your employees. Try to delegate a whole task rather than part of it.

4
MONITOR
Ensure each employee who has been delegated a specific part of the task is performing.

Coaching successfully

There are many different forms of coaching but, in essence, coaching at work is about having a series of conversations with someone to help them to perform better in their job. It is also a highly effective way of motivating them by focusing on their needs.

Coaching on a daily basis

Many people think of coaching as a special form of training undertaken only by a specialist coach. In many cases it is. However, as a manager you will need to understand the principles of coaching and build them into your day-to-day work. You may want to coach someone for a specific task or to prepare them to take on a more senior role. Coach the individuals in your team so they can handle their own work independently. As well as motivating them, this saves you time by enabling them to take responsibility for their own work.

Being a good coach

Assist your employees throughout the duration of the task and keep giving them feedback.

Make observations on someone's behaviour which they may not have noticed themselves.

Enable your staff to find their own way through a problem and suggest practical solutions.

Encourage individuals or teams to take responsibility for a particular task.

Developing your coaching skills

The fundamental skills of coaching are building trust, listening, and questioning. Put the person at their ease to encourage them to talk. While you need to keep the conversation on track, allow them to speak without interruption as far as possible. Ask questions to help maintain their focus and show you are listening. This will also encourage them to think about better ways of doing things and see issues from a wider perspective. Support them as they try implementing their solutions, and give appropriate feedback.

TIP

STIMULATE VIEWPOINTS
By asking a challenging question, you may help your employees to see the issue from a different perspective.

Giving constructive feedback

Feedback is an important part of the coaching process. But make sure it is well-intentioned and constructive. You should also try to make it objective and, above all, not personally hurtful. Try to ensure you back up what you are saying with some evidence. If the individual has no control over something then there is little point in giving them feedback on it.

GIVING APPROPRIATE FEEDBACK

FAST TRACK

OFF TRACK

FAST TRACK	OFF TRACK
Being precise about the feedback	Rushing through what you have to say
Giving the individual time to respond	Giving negative feedback in public
Being constructive	Being uninterested in the way the individual is responding

Chapter 4
Motivating in difficult situations

The environment, processes, and skills of motivation are all important, but some situations will require you to modify your approach. You will need to maintain motivation during change, and in dispersed teams and difficult people.

Motivating during change

Change creates uncertainty for people; it can make them anxious so that they take their eye off the job in hand. However, change is increasingly a requirement for organizations to survive. Being able to motivate during change is therefore an extremely important skill.

Recognizing change

Change is rarely popular, and even seemingly trivial innovations in the organization can cause outrage among your staff. Often this is because people don't understand what is happening. This can be avoided if you think through the change in advance and ask yourself two questions:
• Who will this change affect?
• How will the change look from their point of view?
You will then be able to consult those concerned and ensure they are aware of the benefits the change will bring. This process will ensure they stay motivated.

Identifying the types of change

Change can be categorized as either "hard" or "soft". Hard changes are usually well defined in advance. People can be told what will happen and what is expected of them. In a "soft" change, the details of the change are unknown, and only the direction of the change is clear. The organization has to search for a solution and everyone will have to work through the change together. Major corporate turnarounds often fit this category, as do large-scale cultural change programmes*. The best way to cope with a soft change is to become involved, so you have a chance to shape both the change itself and the future of your team.

*

*Cultural Change Programme
— programme by which the organization tries to change its values and the behaviour of its employees.

Being prepared for the change

Be prepared for any kind of response to change and realize that those affected will respond emotionally, and may at times appear irrational. As a manager you can help them to adjust by:
• Accepting the reaction and responding constructively
• Providing information and support
• Creating new roles and objectives
• Giving people a clear vision of the long-term outcomes.

? ASK YOURSELF... ARE YOU PREPARED TO MOTIVATE YOUR STAFF THROUGH CHANGE?

• Do I need to introduce different motivational goals for the team?
• Do I need to re-set or re-emphasize motivational goals for individuals?
• Will my team lose incentives such as bonuses?
• How can I maintain motivation in spite of this?
• Will the current recognition and reward system be appropriate after the change?
• If not, what changes in the organization will be required to motivate my team in the new way of working?

TIP

SHOW ENDURANCE

Plan for the downturn in performance associated with change, and absorb some of the frustration and anger.

Recognizing the stages of change

More than half a century ago, the sociologist Kurt Lewin identified three major stages of change. These stages will help you to understand the timing of changes, and can be used as a guide for steering people through the process of change.

• **Unfreezing** In this stage you will prepare for change. People will need to recognize the need for the change, and the way things are done will have to be unfrozen, to allow the change to occur. People will be very uncertain during this process.

• **Moving** You will implement the change in this stage by altering working practices, restructuring jobs, or moving people about. People will find everything very new and will need your support and guidance during this process.

• **Refreezing** In this last stage, new ways of working become embedded in the organization. During this phase, people should be finding their feet and starting to move forward. The idea of refreezing is to prevent the organization reverting to its old ways.

The change rollercoaster

PERFORMANCE AND SELF-ESTEEM

Uncertainty

Denial

Blaming others

Blaming self

Despair

TIME

Managing the change rollercoaster

Different people react to change differently, but during major changes, they go through a series of responses that can be characterized as a "rollercoaster ride". This starts with denial, moves on to blaming others, then themselves, which can lead to despair. Self-esteem and performance plummet. However, people then start to test the new environment and ways of working, build confidence, and move on to achieve success. Quite often, once the change has taken place, it is a matter of settling down to the new way of working. You will have to re-establish the culture, rebuild the team morale, and reassure individuals. When the change means employees are made redundant, make the process as painless as possible. Do everything you can to protect their dignity, and help them to take the next steps in their lives.

Performing well

Growing confidence

Testing new ways of working

TIME

Motivating dispersed workers

Developments in technology now enable many people to work from home or in a dispersed team*. In addition, flatter organizational structures mean that even larger organizations have local offices employing just a few people. These arrangements bring benefits, such as flexible working hours, but there are serious implications for motivation.

Working away from the office

*Dispersed team —
*a team based in a
small office out of
immediate contact
with the main body
of the organization.*

For many employees, not working in an office is a dream. For the employer it can mean lower office costs and also better productivity, as staff don't have to spend time commuting to work.

However, the reality can be less appealing. If you work from home, you can feel isolated, making it hard to stay motivated. Individuals miss the buzz of the office, the companionship of colleagues, and the sparking of ideas when they meet other people. In an office, for example, when something goes wrong, you can turn to a colleague who will help you put the problem in perspective.

Recruiting the right candidate

If a job role will be dispersed or home-based, you should look for certain characteristics at the recruitment stage. If someone lacks self-discipline, cannot manage their time well, or appears to need close supervision, they are unlikely to be suitable. You will need to instill loyalty to ensure they are motivated and focused on the goals to be achieved. At the interview, ensure the candidate is prepared for the working environment. At home this means having room for equipment and a quiet environment. For a dispersed team member, it is the lack of direct supervision and support.

Keeping home workers motivated

A crucial aspect of motivating home workers is to take proactive steps to ensure they have everything they need to work effectively. Agree on targets and time scales and monitor them regularly to check that they are on track. Organize regular visits to the main office, such as monthly team meetings, and arrange one-to-one meetings to catch up on progress and to spot any problems before they become too serious. Make sure home- and locally based workers are kept up to date with any new developments, and remain in regular contact – not just by e-mail.

TIP

EXERCISE TRUST

Trust your home workers or dispersed teams. While you need to know the work is being done, you won't motivate people by checking up on them all the time.

Providing support

To keep your dispersed workers motivated, make sure they feel connected to and supported by the organization as a whole. Arrange a thorough induction at your main office and ensure your home workers meet the people they will be e-mailing and speaking to on the phone. You may also need to arrange briefing sessions on working from home. It is particularly important to ensure dispersed teams have all the equipment they need to work effectively. It may be tempting to provide more senior people in head office with the most reliable and expensive IT equipment, but for remote team members, any breakdown is likely to be highly frustrating and time consuming. A comfortable working environment is just as important when working from home or in a small local office.

Depending on the structure, encourage people working near each other to meet up to discuss work. Include home workers and locally based teams in social activities if possible. Look and listen for any signs of stress. Set out precise procedures on who to contact if things go wrong. Make sure "out of sight" is not "out of mind".

Motivating underperformers

At some stage, you will have to manage someone who is not performing well. For the success of your team and the organization, it is important to deal with their problems, as not only will their performance be affected, but they may also disrupt the motivation of your entire team.

HOW TO... DISCUSS PROBLEMS

Inform the individual in advance what you want to discuss.

↓

State your understanding of the situation.

↓

Let the individual explain how they see the issues.

↓

Get them to accept there is a problem if they have not done so.

↓

Encourage them to come up with some solutions.

↓

Arrange a follow-up meeting.

Identifying problems

Everyone makes mistakes occasionally, and while it is important to respond to them constructively, if you do not deal with underperformance your entire team may lose motivation. Get to know what individual team members are capable of and take action when you notice something is going wrong. Watch out for a change in performance. If someone is making more mistakes than usual, you will need to take some action.

Broaching the subject

How you approach the situation will depend on the circumstances. If someone has made a few silly mistakes you may just need to let them know you have noticed, and ask what happened and how it can be avoided in the future. If problems continue, you will need a more considered meeting. Create the same conditions as you would for a performance appraisal meeting – ensure you have privacy, won't be interrupted, and that the individual is comfortable. Prepare for the meeting, and make sure your facts are correct. Think about the problems and possible reasons for them and, if possible, consider them from the perspective of the individual. Try to remain calm and objective at all times and don't digress by discussing other people or issues that don't affect the individual's own performance.

Finding solutions

There may be deep-seated issues behind the obvious reasons for underperformance, and you need to uncover these – otherwise you will only be applying a temporary patch to the problem. Listen very carefully to what is being said, and then probe gently to get underneath the words. In these situations people often blame others or find excuses. Make sure they take responsibility for their own performance. For example, if they say problems are occurring because they are consistently receiving information they need too late, ask why they have not spoken to the person causing the delay.

TIP

BE QUICK TO TAKE ACTION
Ensure you deal with performance problems as soon as they occur. It is very easy to ignore them, especially when you are busy, but doing this will not make them go away.

AGREEING TO SOLUTIONS

PROBLEM	RELEVANT QUESTIONS	POSSIBLE SOLUTIONS
Cannot carry out tasks to the required level	Do they have the right training? Do they have the support they need? Were they recruited into the wrong job?	Provide training or equipment; set objectives for improvement; move them to another role; agree this is not the job for them.
Sudden decline in performance level; making too many silly mistakes	What is causing the lack of concentration? Is it a situation outside work or a problem with a colleague?	Be sympathetic – if necessary let them take some time off work. Work together to find a solution.
Slow decline in performance level	Are they bored with their role? Do they need more challenge to motivate them? Are they overwhelmed by work?	Check whether their role can be broadened or seconded. Help them to manage their workload better.
Timekeeping is bad	Do they have new commitments at home? Are there any personal issues affecting them?	Give them an option of flexible working hours if it helps. Provide professional help if required.
Relationships with colleagues are poor	Are they overloaded with work? Are they showing signs of stress? Is it because of personality clashes?	Train them in "soft" skills such as emotional intelligence. See if they can be moved to a different team.

Motivating a project team

Cross-departmental project teams are common in many organizations. In this situation, you may well find yourself managing a project involving people who don't report to you. As a project leader, your motivational skills will be critical to the project and your own success.

TIP

ENCOURAGE TEAM SPIRIT

Assist and support other members of the team and do not talk behind their backs.

Maintaining the momentum

Every project goes through stages. At first everyone is keen and excited to be involved. Then the work begins. At some stage, problems and setbacks will arise and individuals will become disillusioned and demotivated. This is a critical stage where you, as the project manager, will have to keep the momentum going and make sure people maintain focus and energy. Bring your team together. Remind them that in every project worth doing there are bound to be some setbacks. Bring to mind their earlier successes, explain why the project is still important, and work together to find solutions to the problems. If you still find that they are not giving their best to the project, carefully suggest that there may be someone better equipped to take their role – they will probably receive your message and change their approach.

Sharing success

Motivating a project team is often one of the most difficult tasks. You may not be the line manager of those involved, so you don't have the usual authority and reward mechanisms at your disposal. You may have been given the opportunity to be the project leader, but you will need to share the success with others. If the other team members see you taking all the credit for the project, they will disengage. You need to manage this balance. If the project is successful, you will get recognized, so be generous with your praise along the way. People like their boss to hear good things about them and it only costs you a little time to copy someone into an e-mail saying thank you. Be careful of individuals who "grand stand" and claim greater responsibility for the success of the project than is justified by their contribution.

TIP

MOTIVATE FOR EVERYONE'S BENEFIT

When motivating your project team, think about what benefits your team can expect from succeeding.

Driving project teams forward

EXUDE ENTHUSIASM
Make the measures of success very explicit and exude your enthusiasm for the project.

GIVE VISIBILITY
Explain that being part of the project will bring people to the notice of their seniors, which can help their careers.

HAVE FUN
Make the project interesting and fun so that people participate and contribute willingly.

USE PEER PRESSURE
Involve the whole team to help you apply pressure on any member who is underperforming.

BE FIRM
Threaten to remove an underperforming team member – and make sure you can back up your threat if necessary.

Motivating teams

Having a group of motivated individuals in your department is a good start, but you won't be really successful unless you have a motivated team. People in teams bounce ideas off each other and work together to achieve better results than individuals working alone.

Painting a picture of the future

One of the most important motivators for a team is having a common goal that each individual has a genuine commitment to achieving. Paint a picture, either graphically or in words, describing what success will look like. Be enthusiastic about achieving it. Talk about your people's role in delivering the success and allude to the benefits of being successful and what success will feel like.

Elements of an effective team

A GOOD LEADER
Having a leader who applies, at team level, all the lessons for motivating each individual on the team.

PEOPLE WHO CAN WORK TOGETHER
Consisting of people who respect fellow team members and are allowed to question and express dissent on occasions.

Creating a sense of belonging

The sense of "belonging" is a very important motivator and, while this does develop naturally when a team has been together over a period of time, a good manager will speed up the process and ensure it is maintained by, for example, celebrating success. Make sure that each member of your team knows how they fit into the working of the whole organization.

Setting benchmarks

At times, seemingly motivated and well-established teams can become complacent. One way of avoiding this is to take your team on benchmarking* visits. Find an organization that does something very well and go and visit them. You will find many organizations are only too happy to do this, particularly if they can "benchmark" with you in return.

*Benchmarking — the systematic process of comparing your performance with others'.

GOOD COMMUNICATION PROCESSES
Establishing free-flowing information within the team and good networks and contacts outside.

OPEN TO ALTERNATIVES
Considering all options and opening the team to external criticism, or ensuring that you have at least one respected critic on the team.

COMMON UNDERSTANDING
Having complete awareness of the team's goals along with an understanding of the role and contribution of each team member.

Bringing it all together

Motivation is part art and part science. You need to understand the theory and apply it in practice with feeling and sincerity. Motivation is like a chain – it is only as strong as its weakest link. It ceases to become effective if any of the links are missing.

GAIN YOUR STAFF'S TRUST

Take genuine interest in your employees – support them in a professional crisis and look after their long-term career interests to keep them motivated beyond the short term.

Keeping your staff motivated

Motivating people in the short term is relatively easy. But when you have to motivate people over the longer term, enthusiasm alone won't work. To do this you have to create a culture that is conducive to success, balance organizational and personal goals, and ensure people are genuinely interested in the success of the organization. To keep people motivated over the long term, you must be trusted as a leader. You will need to support people by giving them the tools and resources to do the job, helping them overcome obstacles that may get in the way, developing their skills, and rewarding success. Being a good motivator will not only help your organization but will boost your career too.

Making each job worthwhile

All jobs in your organization are important – if not, they should be eliminated immediately. Ensure that every job is done well, from dealing with customers, to producing high quality products and keeping the facilities clean. Achieving this requires all managers and supervisors in the organization to engage, motivate, and direct their staff. As a manager it is your responsibility to make the organization a great place for people to work and to encourage them to contribute to the success of the organization.

Tracking performance

TIP

REVIEW PERFORMANCE

Every six months you should stop and reflect on your team's performance. Ask yourself where you are succeeding, and where you are falling short.

Always ensure that you and your team are developing, learning, and moving on. You will achieve success only when your team has a positive perception of you, and the organizational environment is favourable and supportive. Use the scorecard featured below to track your performance in motivating people. Think about the elements of the scorecard as the links in a chain. Each link has to be strong to give the chain strength, so use the scorecard to guide where you need to focus your attention. It is important that you plan to strengthen any weaknesses that may appear. You could even use the scorecard with trusted team members or colleagues to help you develop your abilities and become a great motivator.

Motivation scorecard

HOW MOTIVATED IS MY STAFF?
Does my team:
• show enthusiasm?
• work well with each other?
• go the extra mile?
• perform well?
• achieve the goals that are set for them?

HOW WELL AM I PERCEIVED?
Do I:
• have the trust of my staff?
• have a good working relationship with my team?
• support my colleagues?
• appear approachable?
• motivate people well?

HOW SUPPORTIVE IS THE ENVIRONMENT?
Do we:
• have the opportunity to do well?
• have the tools to do our job?
• have the support of our bosses and colleagues?

HOW ARE WE LEARNING?
Have I:
• developed my own skills and abilities?
• helped someone to learn a new skill in the last month?
• helped someone get promoted this year?

Index

Acknowledgments

Author's acknowledgments
We would like to acknowledge and thank Mike's friends and colleagues at the Centre for Business Performance, Cranfield School of Management, for their support and ideas incorporated into this book, and Graham, Georgie, Cynthia, Pat, and Min for their motivation.

Publisher's acknowledgments
The publisher would like to thank Margaret Parrish and Charles Wills for co-ordinating Americanization.